Sensational Settings

OVER 80 WAYS TO ARRANGE YOUR QUILT BLOCKS

Joan Hanson

That Patchwork Place®

Contents

CREDITS

Editor .... Barbara Weiland
Copy Editor .... Liz McGehee
Text and Cover
  Design .... Joanne Lauterjung
Typesetting .... Karin LaFramboise
Photography .... Brent Kane
Illustrations .... André Samson

Sensational Settings: Over 80 Ways to Arrange Your Quilt Blocks©
©1993 by Joan Hanson

That Patchwork Place, Inc., PO Box 118, Bothell, WA 98041-0118 USA

Printed in the United States of America
98 97 96 95 94   6 5 4

**Library of Congress
Cataloging-in-Publication Data**
Hanson, Joan,
    Sensational Settings : over 80 ways to arrange your quilt blocks / Joan Hanson.
      p. cm.
    ISBN 1-56477-018-4 :
    1. Patchwork—Patterns. 2. Quilting—Patterns. I. Title.
TT835.H337 1993
746.9'7—dc20   92-35396
                                          CIP

ACKNOWLEDGMENTS

A special thank you to my husband, Jim, and sons, Derek and Mark, for cheerfully tolerating hastily thrown-together dinners and many household chores left undone while I worked on this book. I appreciate their patience.

I am also grateful for many quilting friends, including Julie Stewart, Mary Hickey, Cleo Nollette, Nancy Martin, and Janet Kime, who were always there to offer encouragement and support when I needed it the most. You've all given the gift of friendship and shown what our foremothers knew all along—that quilters are truly special people.

I am also indebted to the hardworking and skilled staff of That Patchwork Place, who have been so helpful and have made this book a reality.

My thanks also to the Hershey Company for always having a "kiss" ready for me when I needed one.

We all know one when we see one, a quilt that reaches out and speaks to us, asking us to linger and enjoy its beauty for just a little longer. In this book we will explore a variety of ways to set quilt blocks together in a pleasing overall design to create a stunning quilt that is a joy to behold.

Coming up with an idea for a quilt happens in many different ways. Perhaps you have received a set of friendship blocks that need to be set or inherited some from a relative. You may have won a set of blocks at a guild meeting or made a set of sampler blocks in a class. Maybe a beautiful block in a book or magazine caught your eye and you know you *have* to make a quilt using that pattern. You might have fabrics in your collection that you want to use in a quilt or perhaps you want to make a baby quilt or a wedding quilt for a special friend. A collection of fabrics from various trips would make a wonderful travel quilt. Or, you may simply have a bed in your home that needs a quilt.

Turning your initial enthusiasm into a successful quilt takes some thought and planning. To me, designing the setting and choosing the fabrics are among the most exciting and important steps in producing a stunning quilt. Following the step-by-step plan presented in this book will enable you to start cutting and stitching your way to the quilt of your dreams. Sometimes, you will decide not to make a particular quilt after working your way through the planning stage. Consider the time well spent as you will have made that decision before investing your time and fabric in a quilt that might have been a disappointment.

When you start a project, you will probably have one or more "givens" with which to work. Perhaps the finished quilt needs to be a certain size to cover a particular bed or wall space, or you have a given number of blocks and want to end up with a quilt of a particular size. You can plan a quilt setting to stretch blocks to cover a bigger area or squeeze them into a smaller area.

Many variables come into play when you decide how to set blocks into a quilt. Some blocks must be set horizontally, such as House blocks, while other blocks are designed for a diagonal set, also called "on point." Many Basket blocks are designed on point, for example. A variety of blocks, such as Star blocks, can be oriented either horizontally or diagonally with dramatically different results. As a general rule, remember that horizontal lines are calming and restful, while diagonal lines give movement and add drama to your design.

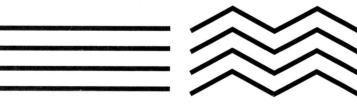

Peaceful   Dramatic

The choice is up to you. Don't hesitate to branch out and try setting a quilt in a way you haven't tried before. It's easier than you may think!

As you look through the settings that follow, consider them as a beginning to spark your own ideas. Try combining elements of several of these setting ideas to come up with your own variations. Remember, there are no hard and fast rules here. Some of the best quilt settings are just waiting to be tried, so don't hesitate to break out and reach for them.

3

General Terms

There are many more elements besides quilt blocks that make up a quilt. Since these terms will be used throughout this book, it is important to become familiar with them by studying the illustration and definitions that follow. Alternate names for terms are given in parentheses.

Common Quilt Terms

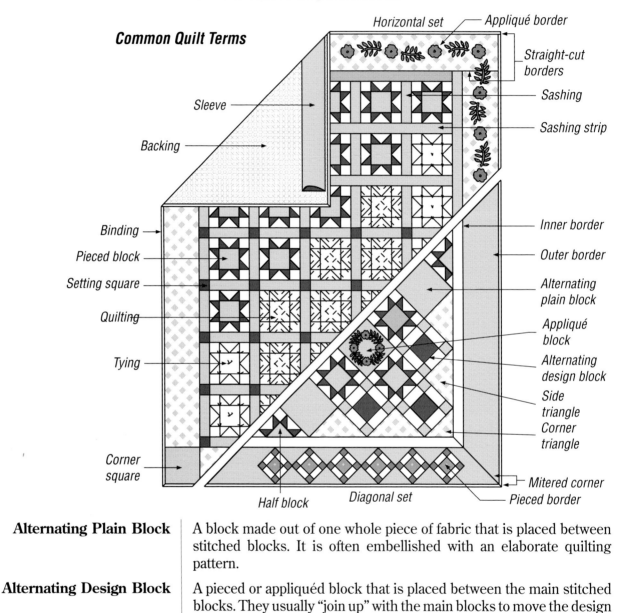

Alternating Plain Block	A block made out of one whole piece of fabric that is placed between stitched blocks. It is often embellished with an elaborate quilting pattern.
Alternating Design Block	A pieced or appliquéd block that is placed between the main stitched blocks. They usually "join up" with the main blocks to move the design across the quilt.
Appliqué Block	A design made up of small (usually curved) pieces that are stitched by hand or machine onto a larger background block that forms a unit of the quilt top.
Appliqué Border	A design made up of small (usually curved) pieces that are stitched by hand or machine onto long strips that form the border of the quilt.
Backing (lining)	A large piece of fabric that covers the back of a quilt. It may have to be seamed together from more than one piece of fabric for a large quilt.

A layer inside the quilt, sandwiched between the quilt top and the quilt backing. It is usually a fluffy polyester, cotton, wool, or silk (or some combination thereof) that adds warmth and texture to the quilt. — **Batting**

A strip of fabric, cut on either the straight of grain or the bias, that is stitched to the edge of a quilt to cover the raw edges. — **Binding**

Usually a square or rectangular design unit that is pieced or appliquéd. Typically, quilt tops are made by repeating one or more quilt block designs in a pleasing arrangement. — **Block**

The area surrounding the main body of the quilt top. It acts like the frame on a picture to enhance the design. It may be a pieced or appliquéd design, or it may be made of one or more strips of fabric of varying widths. — **Border**

A square of fabric sometimes used to join adjacent border strips. — **Corner Square**

A quarter-square triangle used to fill in the four corners of a diagonally set quilt before the borders (if any) are added. — **Corner Triangle**

A design arranged so the blocks are pieced together in diagonal rows, with side and corner triangles added to complete the rows. — **Diagonal Set** (on-point set)

Half of a design unit used to fill in at the side, top, or bottom of a diagonally set quilt to create a straight edge. — **Half Block**

A design arranged so that the blocks and other components are oriented horizontally and vertically. — **Horizontal Set** (straight set)

A point where three seams intersect at an angle to form a "Y." — **Mitered Corner** (set-in corner)

Small pieces of fabric in various shapes stitched together by hand or machine to form a larger design. — **Pieced Block**

A design made up of small shapes stitched together into long strips that form the border of the quilt. — **Pieced Border**

The upper layer of a quilt that is usually appliquéd or pieced to form the overall design. It can be made up of any combination of blocks, sashing, setting squares, and borders. — **Quilt Top**

A strip of fabric sewn between two rows of blocks. — **Sashing Strip** (lattice strip)

Strips of fabric sewn between blocks. — **Sashing** (lattice)

A square of fabric at the intersection of two sashings. It may be one piece of fabric, or pieced or appliquéd. — **Setting Square** (corner post, set square, sashing square)

A half-square triangle used to fill in at the side, top, or bottom of a diagonally set quilt to create a straight edge. These should be cut so the straight grain of the fabric is on the long side of the triangle to add stability to the quilt and prevent stretching along the edges. — **Side Triangle** (edge triangle)

A tube attached to the backing at the top edge of a quilt so that a hanging rod or dowel can be inserted. — **Sleeve** (rod pocket)

A border that is applied to the quilt top in two steps. First, border strips are stitched to two opposite sides (usually the longest sides). Then the remaining borders are stitched to the quilt and already-attached borders. The two sets of borders butt into each other rather than meeting at an angle, as in a mitered corner. — **Straight-Cut Border**

Quilt Settings

CONSIDER THIS SETTING FOR:

☐ Log Cabin, Double Wedding Ring, Drunkard's Path, and Kaleidoscope
☐ Blocks that form a secondary design when joined together
☐ Appliqué blocks that "float" on the background

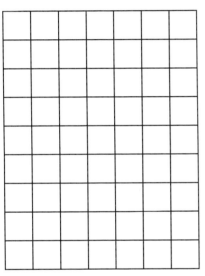

Side-by-side Horizontal Setting

Side-by-side Diagonal Setting

Side By Side

This is probably the most used and overused setting because it is easy and the first one that comes to mind. Just line up your blocks in neat rows and sew them together. We are used to organizing things in this way, but it is a way to get a set of blocks made into a quilt quickly without giving a lot of thought to how they could be set to their best advantage.

However, many blocks gain an unexpected graphic punch when set side by side. Many times, a secondary pattern emerges as the boundary of one block blurs together with its neighboring blocks, causing a new and unexpected design to appear. Try changing the colors in the blocks from the center to the edges of your quilt (light to dark), or change the background fabric in each block to set off each one.

Another option along these same lines is to change the color arrangement in every other block. If a block is asymmetrical, such as a Log Cabin block, try turning the blocks in different directions to create a variety of results. The old-time favorite settings for Log Cabin blocks—Streak of Lightning, Sunshine and Shadows, Barn Raising, Straight Furrows, Light and Dark, and Pinwheel—are accomplished this way.

Appliqué blocks that "float" on the background fabric are very effective set side by side. If you are considering this setting, try placing your blocks on point to see how this affects the look of your blocks. Many blocks take on a new and dramatic look when set this way.

Many blocks, such as this 54-40 or Fight block, change dramatically when rotated from a horizontal to a diagonal setting.

The same block set side by side becomes more interesting when the background fabric changes from block to block.

This Pinwheel block forms a secondary pinwheel when blocks are set side by side.

Ocean Waves blocks are usually set in a side-by-side setting so that the design flows over the quilt. (This diagonal setting with two corner blocks accommodates seventeen blocks.)

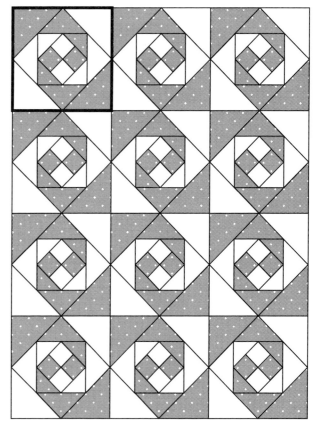

The Snail's Trails multiply when blocks are joined side by side.

This Rail Fence–Flying Geese variation creates a woven look when the blocks alternate directions, adding movement and drama.

This Anvil block not only changes direction with every other block, but the color scheme changes from block to block as well.

This is another example of an appliqué block that floats on its background fabric. The diagonal set allows space in the side and corner triangles for a fancy quilting design.

The outer flowers on this appliqué wreath create a secondary design when they meet in the corners. The wreaths "float" on their plain block backgrounds.

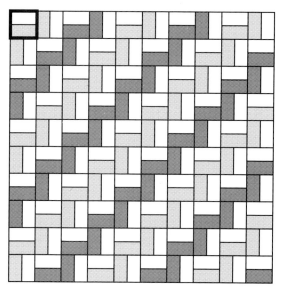

*Rotating a simple Rail Fence block in a
side-by-side setting creates a zigzag design.*

*Alternating the direction of these Spool blocks sets off each block.
(See color photo on page 29.)*

Barn Raising

Straight Furrows

Light and Dark

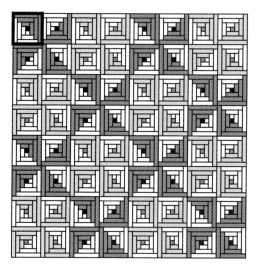

Pinwheel

Endless setting variations are possible when you change the orientation of the light and dark sides of Log Cabin blocks.

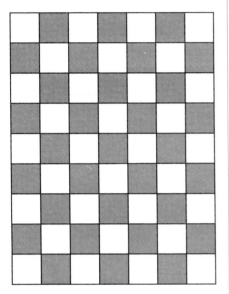

CONSIDER THIS SETTING FOR:

☐ Ninepatch or other designs that connect at the corners to give diagonal movement
☐ Complex pieced or appliqué blocks
☐ Stretching a few blocks into a bigger quilt
☐ Creating a space to show off elaborate quilting

Alternating Plain Blocks

If you have a limited number of blocks and want to stretch them into a larger quilt, alternating your design blocks with a plain block can do the trick. Just remember that all those plain blocks will probably require a greater amount of quilting. The time you don't spend piecing additional blocks will be spent quilting later.

Many blocks connect visually at the corners and add diagonal movement to a quilt when alternated with a plain block, such as a simple Ninepatch alternating with a plain block that has the same background fabric. When you use the same background fabric for the plain block as you do in your design blocks, the design blocks appear to "float" on the surface of the quilt.

Plain blocks cut from a floral print or a dark solid might also be a good choice for setting off your blocks to their best advantage. An easy way to get the look of a medallion setting is to change the color of the alternating plain block from the edges to the center. When you are using alternating blocks, you will want an odd number of blocks in each row and an odd number of rows so that you end up with the same type of block in each corner.

Many lovely appliqué blocks are set with alternating plain blocks. Elaborate quilting enhances the plain blocks. This can be a stunning combination.

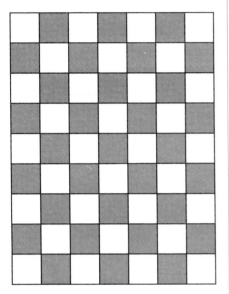

Side-by-side Horizontal Setting with Alternating Plain Blocks

Side-by-side Diagonal Setting with Alternating Plain Blocks

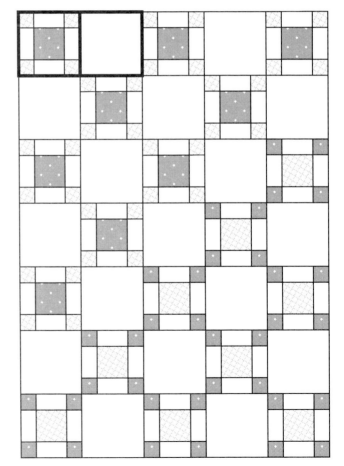

Puss in the Corner also connects in the corners, wherever the lights and darks are placed.

Small blocks can be grouped into larger Four Patch or Ninepatch blocks with alternating plain blocks, then combined with a large alternating block.

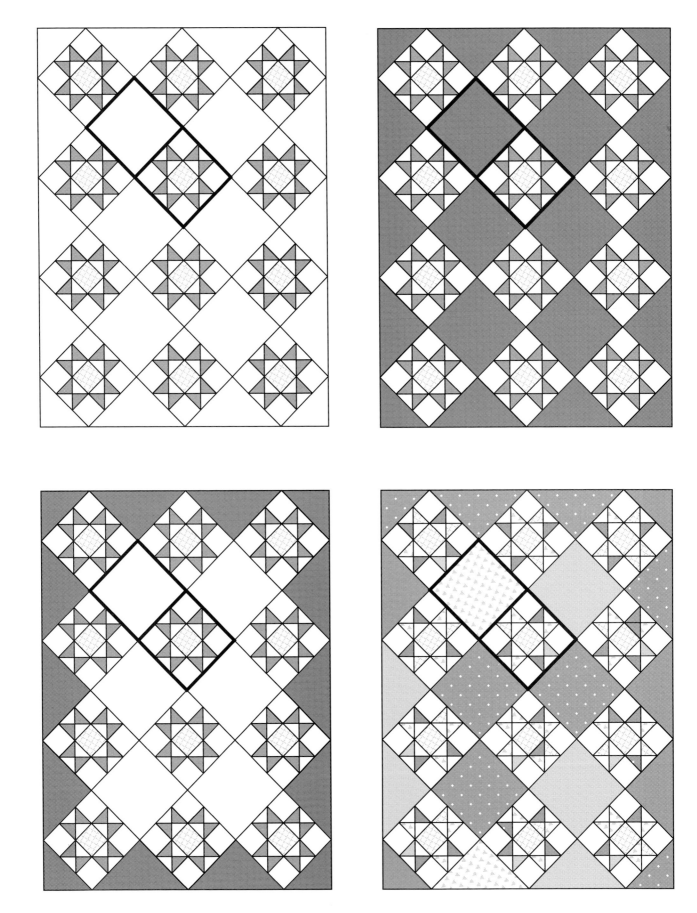

This Star block takes on a variety of looks, depending on the fabric used in the alternating block.

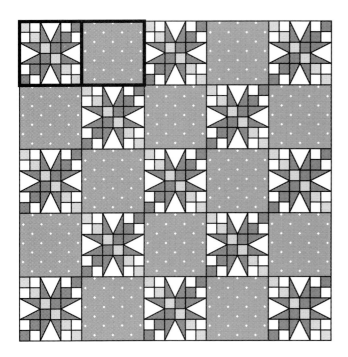

The simplicity of Sister's Choice makes it special. The plain alternating blocks can be filled with fine hand quilting.

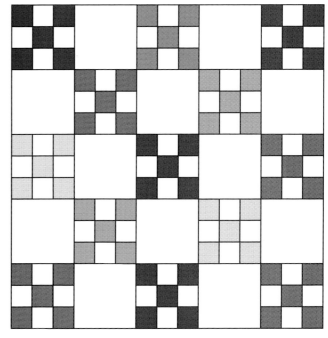

A Single Irish Chain is a very effective, yet simple, example of using an alternating plain block to form a pleasing overall design that connects at the corners.

Appliqué blocks and elaborate hand quilting seem to complement each other. To highlight quilting stitches, use a solid color for the alternating blocks, or a print to conceal them.

These baskets float in the center and are framed by contrasting fabric in the side and corner triangles.

CONSIDER THIS SETTING FOR:

□ Irish Chain or other "A" block/ "B" block designs
□ Appliqué blocks
□ Complex blocks that relate to a simple companion block

Alternating Design Blocks

Many interesting combinations happen when two different pieced or appliqué blocks are combined. Usually one of the blocks is more complex than the other and, for pieced blocks, both blocks have the same divisions, such as in Ninepatch, sixteen-patch, or twenty-five-patch, so that some of the intersections line up and carry the eye across the quilt.

Examples of some simple alternating blocks include Snowball, Churn Dash, and Puss in the Corner. Some patterns, such as Irish Chain, use an "A" block that alternates with a "B" block to create a pleasing overall design. If you are setting an appliqué quilt, consider using a simple pieced or appliqué design that relates to the main blocks for a change.

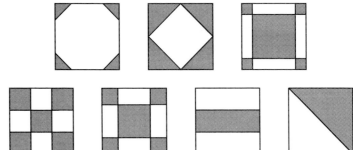

These simple pieced blocks can be used as alternating blocks.

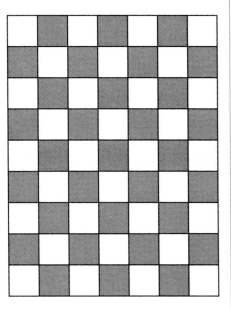

Side-by-side Horizontal Setting with Alternating Design Blocks

Side-by-side Diagonal Setting with Alternating Design Blocks

Double Irish Chain relies on an alternating block with a square in each corner to carry the design across the surface.

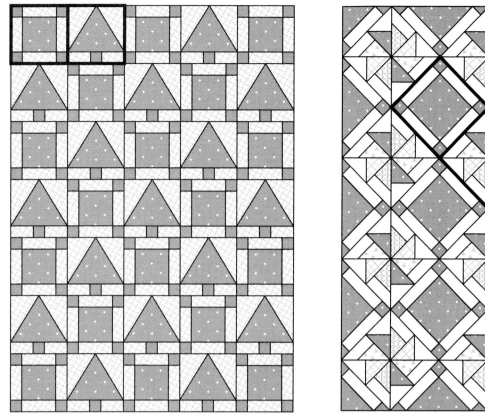

Although one design is set horizontally and the other is set diagonally, these two designs both use a Puss in the Corner as an alternating block with background fabric matching the background fabric in the main block.

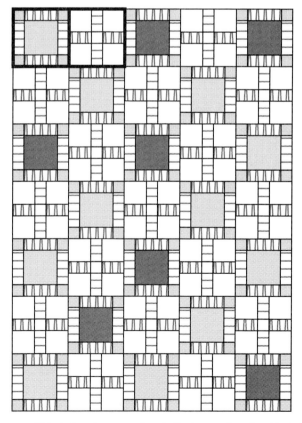

This design also uses a Puss in the Corner alternating block, but since the segments are shaded differently, the effect is quite different.

Snowball blocks combined with other blocks create diagonal movement across the quilt surface.

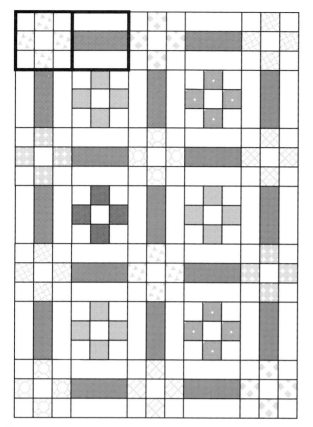

These two very simple blocks combine with very satisfying results. (Note how the lights and darks change in the Ninepatch blocks in each quilt.)

A diagonal setting carries the eye across the surface of this scrap quilt.

This charming scrap quilt uses a diagonal setting to carry the eye across the surface.

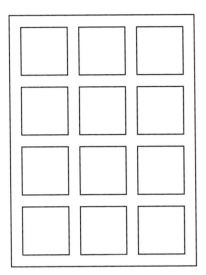

CONSIDER THIS SETTING FOR:

☐ Sampler or friendship blocks
☐ Blocks that stand on their own
☐ Picture blocks, such as Basket blocks

Side-by-side Horizontal Setting with Sashing

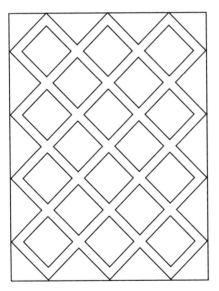

Side-by-side Diagonal Setting with Sashing

Simple Sashing

Many blocks look best if they are set apart and are allowed to stand on their own without interfering with neighboring blocks. Sampler blocks are often set with simple sashing between blocks to add a unifying element to blocks that don't hold together on their own. This works especially well if the sashing fabric contains colors from each of the blocks.

Experiment with the width of sashing—narrow sashing lets the design jump easily from block to block, while wider sashing sets them apart. Wider sashing can also stretch a limited number of blocks into a larger quilt.

Using sashing that matches the background fabric in the blocks causes the blocks to "float" on the surface of the quilt. Using a printed sashing fabric helps to blur the seams, while a solid fabric shows off a beautiful quilting design.

When you are cutting sashing, cut short strips the same size as your block to fit between the blocks in each row and then cut long sashing strips to join the rows. When you are assembling the rows, make sure that the blocks and sashing strips line up from row to row.

When sashings match the background fabric in the blocks, the blocks are separated and appear to float.

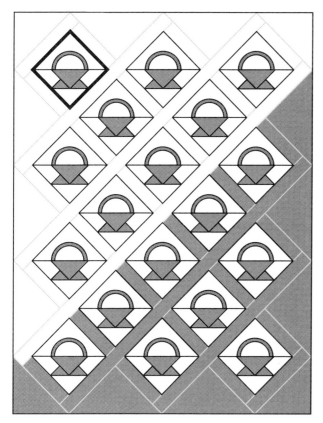

Changing the sashing fabric gives two different looks to these blocks.

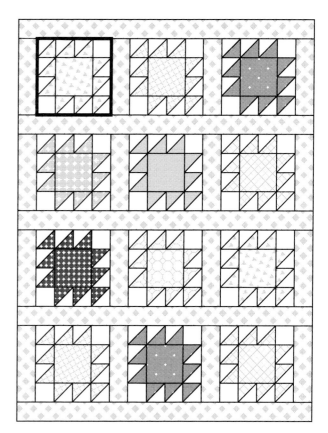

Wide sashing in a print helps to unify these scrappy Anvil blocks.

This appliqué sampler is held together with a narrow printed sashing.

These sampler blocks are surrounded by a narrow frame (to bring the blocks all up to the same size) and then a wide sashing.

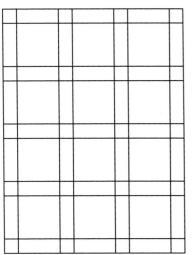

*Side-by-side Horizontal Setting
with Sashing Strips and Setting Squares*

*Side-by-side Diagonal Setting
with Sashing Strips and Setting Squares*

Sashing and Setting Squares

Once you've completed a set of blocks, piecing sashings and setting squares may seem like too much trouble, but they can really enhance the look of your blocks. Setting squares help connect blocks to carry the eye across the quilt surface. Sometimes, they simply add more design interest. You can also piece the sashing and/or setting squares to contribute to the overall design.

You may want to design a sashing that joins up with the intersections in your blocks (Ninepatch, sixteen-patch, twenty-five-patch), and helps join the blocks together. Try sashing that uses the background fabric with a contrasting setting square to give a floating effect. Or strip-piece the sashing, using two strips of the background fabric with another fabric. Place the background strips on either side of the contrasting strip. This opens up the visual space around each block.

Try taking a design element from the block, either pieced or appliqué, and use it in the setting square in its original size or reduced to a smaller scale. Four Patches, Ninepatches, and Puss in the Corner are good choices for pieced setting squares. Sometimes, the sashings and the borders can blend together for an effective look. Try repeating the setting-square design in the corners of the border, for example.

Setting squares in each of these quilts match the background of the blocks. Wider contrasting sashing separates the pieced blocks, while the narrow sashing in the appliqué sampler draws the blocks together.

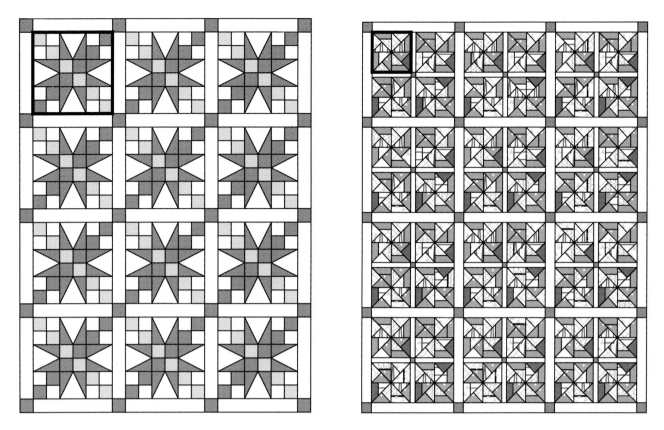

These two quilts have sashings that match the background of the blocks and setting squares that contrast. In the quilt on the right, above, note how four Pinwheel blocks are joined together with narrow sashing and setting squares into a larger block, and then wider sashing and setting squares are used to join them into rows.

Detail of Garden Path sashing and setting square

This setting is called Garden Path and is usually used with floral appliqué blocks. It can be used for either a horizontal or diagonal setting.

There are several alternatives for ending the rows of sashing and setting squares on a diagonal setting. The appliqué quilt (above, left) has whole setting squares along the outside edges. The setting squares are cut in half along the outside edges on the Star quilt (above, right). The Basket quilt (right) was designed with the sashing and setting squares on the diagonal in the center of the quilt instead of centering the block at the corner as in the Star quilt (above, right). In the pieced Star quilt (above, right), the setting squares were cut in half at the outside edges.

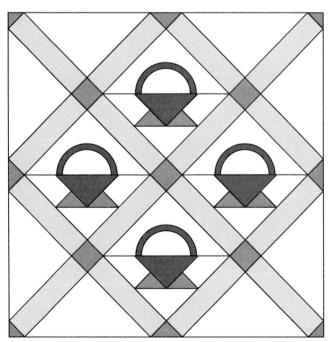

Ninepatch setting squares combine with pieced sashing to surround blocks in several different ways in these three quilts (above and left).

Detail of Variable Star sashing and setting square

The pieced sashing and setting squares in this Variable Star quilt repeat the star design, only in a slightly smaller scale.

A plain sashing and a pieced setting square that repeat an element found in the block design help to carry the design across each of the quilts shown here.

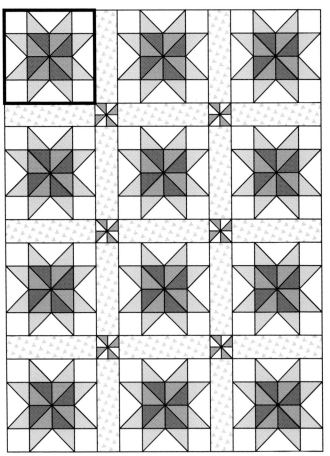

Too Fruity by Joan W. Hanson, 1992, Seattle, Washington, 58" x 75".
Star sampler blocks are surrounded by two different types of frames so that
some stars are set horizontally while the rest are set diagonally.

Spring Baskets I by Joan W. Hanson and Needle & I Guild Members, 1986, Seattle, Washington, 42" x 58".
When these diagonally oriented blocks are set side by side, eight blocks are required.

Spring Baskets II by Joan W. Hanson and Needle & I Guild Members, 1988, Seattle, Washington, 58" x 58".
When the same Basket blocks are alternated with a plain block, nine Basket blocks are needed.
There is plenty of room for hand quilting in the plain blocks.

Class Heroes by Joan W. Hanson and the Fourth Grade Class of Jody Lemke, View Ridge Elementary School, 1992, Seattle, Washington, 62" x 76". This setting was designed to accommodate the blocks made by the twenty-six students in the class. Framing the blocks with corner triangles of two alternating colors forms a star around the heroes.

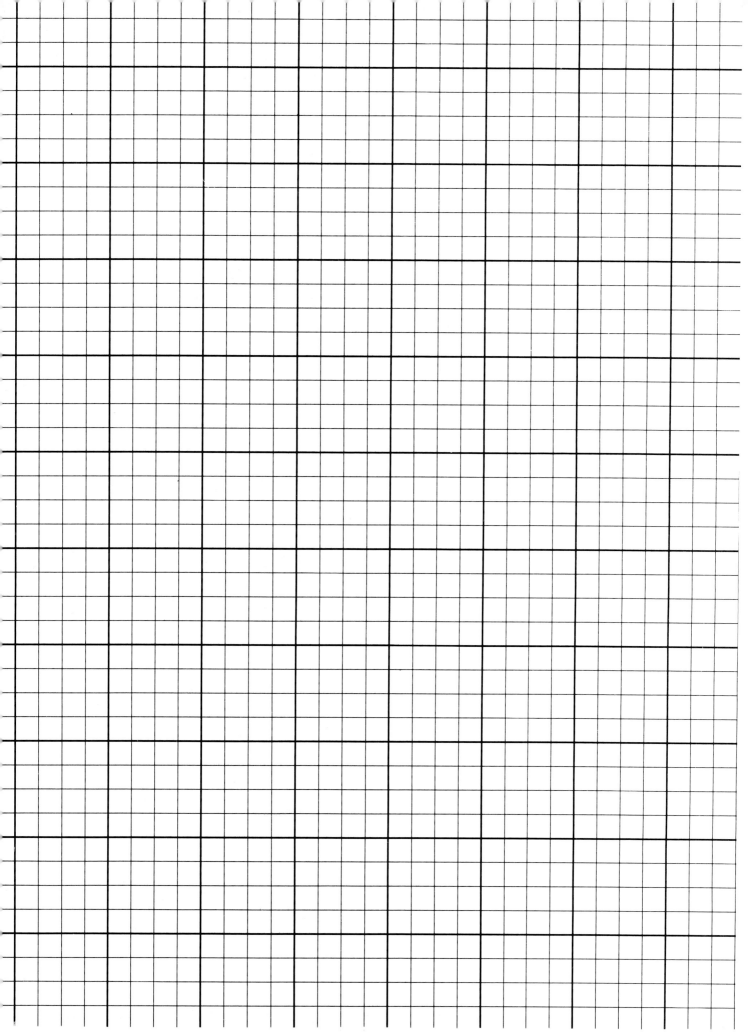

Friendship Spools by Joan W. Hanson and fifty-six quilter friends, 1988, Seattle, Washington, 54" x 60". In this side-by-side setting, the spool blocks alternate directions so that they appear to float on a light background.

The Gilded Lily by Joan W. Hanson, 1987, Seattle, Washington, 48" x 56".
This quilt commemorates the Washington State Centennial. The four center blocks are named for the state of Washington. Since each one has twelve set-in corners, I only made four and decided on a medallion setting.

Garden Girls by Dorothy Everett Whitelaw and Joan W. Hanson, 1930s, 1989, Seattle, Washington, 41" x 45". My mother made these blocks as a young girl. As a surprise for her seventieth birthday, I made her this quilt. I chose a pieced sashing with pieced setting squares to set it, using soft shades of light blue so that the blocks wouldn't be overwhelmed.

Star Light, Star Bright by Joan W. Hanson, 1986, Seattle, Washington, 54" x 72". Scrappy pink stars and scrappy green Puss in the Corner blocks alternate to form this twinkling design.

Dutchman's Puzzle by Tecla Coffee Rippeteau, 1898, 75" x 88". The diagonal strippy setting adds movement to these blocks.

Framed Blocks

This is one of my favorite settings because you can use it to standardize the size of blocks that would otherwise be difficult to join together. This setting is great for sampler or friendship blocks or any other group of blocks that are not all the same size and/or shape.

You can standardize the size of blocks that are each a different size by adding an oversized border or "frame" to each block, then trimming them all down to the same size. The width of the frame may vary slightly. But you will be working with blocks that will be easy to join.

There are several frame variations from which to choose. Use the same fabric to go halfway around each block, then choose another fabric to frame the other half of each block. Then alternate the blocks. Or, use a dark fabric for two adjoining sides and a light fabric for the remaining two sides. This requires that you miter the corners, but when all the blocks are put together, it creates the illusion that light is shining on your quilt. Attic Windows is a variation of this idea.

Another possibility is to add sashing and setting squares to each block. When these blocks are joined, a Four Patch is created at each intersection. (Your blocks must be a consistent size for this strategy to work.) Add triangles to each side of your blocks to frame them and change their orientation from horizontal to diagonal or the other way around. Try framing your blocks, then combining them with sashing and set squares for a more elaborate effect.

CONSIDER THIS SETTING FOR:

☐ Sampler blocks
☐ Friendship blocks
☐ Blocks that didn't come out quite the same size

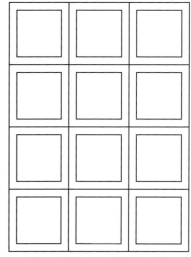

Framed Blocks in Side-by-side Horizontal Setting

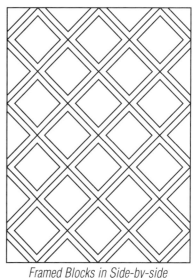

Framed Blocks in Side-by-side Diagonal Setting

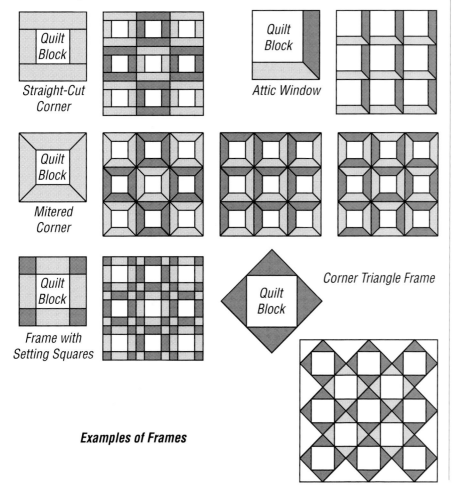

Examples of Frames

Narrow framing sets off the blocks, which appear to "float" between the wider sashing strips.

Two prints alternate to frame these appliqué blocks.

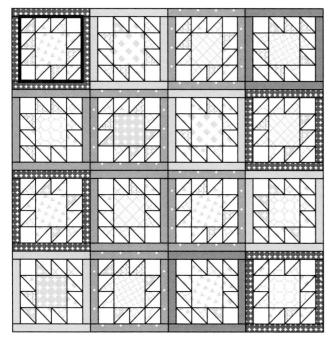

These scrappy blocks are each framed with a different print to add to the scrappy look.

Each block is framed with a light fabric on opposite sides and a dark fabric on the other two sides, which gives a three-dimensional effect.

Blocks in both of these quilts are framed with corner triangles in alternating colors. Notice that the appliqué Basket quilt started out with diagonal blocks and became a horizontal setting, while the appliqué Heart blocks change from a horizontal orientation to a diagonal.

Two-color frames with Four-Patch setting squares tie these sampler blocks together.

This quilt combines simple framing and corner triangle framing. This would be a good choice for sampler blocks or any group of blocks where some of the blocks are oriented horizontally and some are oriented diagonally.

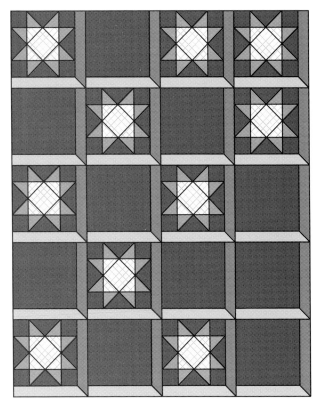

Attic Windows frame these Star blocks. Add blank window blocks at random to stretch fewer pieced blocks into a larger quilt or to set an odd number of blocks together.

This quilt combines two framing options, a box-shaped frame and a simple frame in two alternating colors.

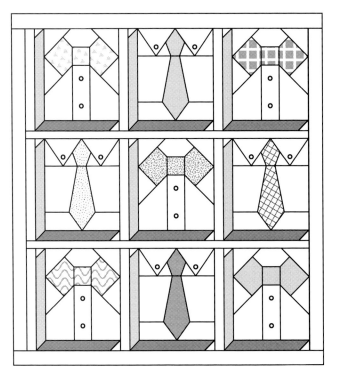

A dark box-shaped frame surrounds two adjacent sides of these shirt blocks to give the illusion of shirt boxes. Simple sashing separates the blocks.

Stripped Sets with Sashing

In this setting, your blocks touch each other in one direction and are separated by sashing in the other direction. For horizontally set quilts, the sashing can run crosswise or lengthwise.

If the sashing runs crosswise, it creates a "landscape" for houses, bunnies, cats, cars, trains, or other objects in your quilt. Your sashing could be grass, sidewalk, highway, flowers, or a train track, for example.

An example of the sashing running lengthwise would be a Flying Geese quilt. Keep your eyes open for lovely vine-type floral prints that could be used for a vertical sashing treatment. When this idea is carried over to a diagonal setting, it produces a zigzag effect. To do this, every other row is moved up half a block, and an odd number of rows is used to balance each side. This is a good way to set an odd number of blocks, such as seven, eleven, or eighteen blocks.

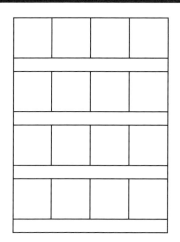

CONSIDER THIS SETTING FOR:

- Flying Geese blocks
- Picture blocks, such as trees, houses, bunnies, cats, cars, and trains
- Adding movement to a diagonal setting

Vertical sashing in strippy quilts can be wide or narrow, with blocks set horizontally or on the diagonal with side triangles.

Side-by-side Stripped Setting with Horizontal Sashing

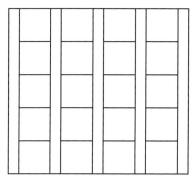

Side-by-side Stripped Setting with Vertical Sashing

Diagonal Setting Creating a Zigzag

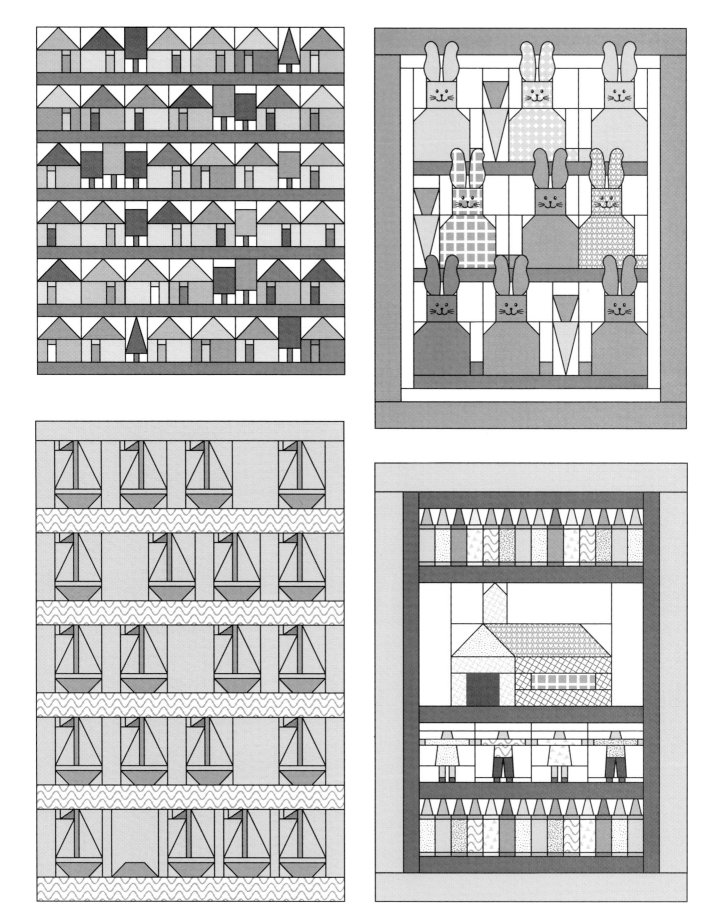

Crosswise sashing creates a landscape for houses, bunnies, boats, kids, and crayons.

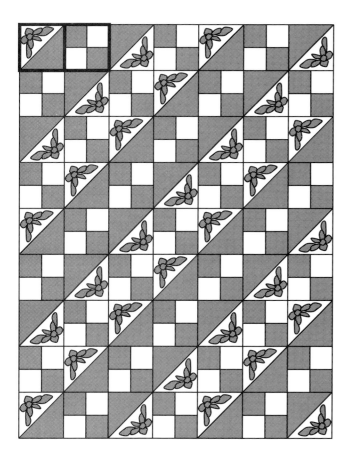

Technically, these quilts fall into other categories, but they have such a strong strippy look, I included them here as a strippy variation.

A diagonal strippy setting has diagonally set blocks in rows that begin and end with a half block to create a zigzag effect. Side and corner triangles complete the set.

Medallion Sets

This setting has many different variations. Included here are some basic ideas to use as a starting point. Medallions usually have one or more blocks as a central focus. From there, borders, blocks, or other elements are added. These elements could be pieced or appliquéd, or a combination of both.

Often, the various elements switch from a diagonal setting to a horizontal setting, creating the illusion that one part is placed on top of another. This is a good option for a large central block, or if you don't want to make the same block over and over.

There are many variations on the medallion setting, but I have included examples that use multiples of blocks of the same size. Perhaps more than any of the other settings, this one takes some planning with graph paper, but the results are well worth the effort!

If you are switching from diagonal to horizontal orientation in your design, it may be helpful to cut out your design that is oriented in one direction and paste it onto a new sheet of graph paper when you change to the other orientation, so that you are always working with graph paper that lines up with your design. For example, if the center blocks are set diagonally and corner triangles are added, then more blocks set horizontally, use graph paper oriented in the same way as the blocks, diagonally and horizontally.

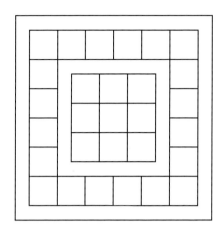

Straight-Set Medallion

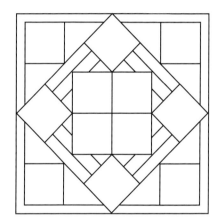

Diagonally Set Medallion

Medallion settings tend to end up square, but adding a row of blocks or an extra border to the top and bottom edges changes the shape to a rectangle. (See color photo of Gilded Lily on page 30.)

Four appliqué blocks form the center of this medallion setting with eight more blocks used around the edges.

Twelve appliqué blocks surround a large central block in this medallion setting.

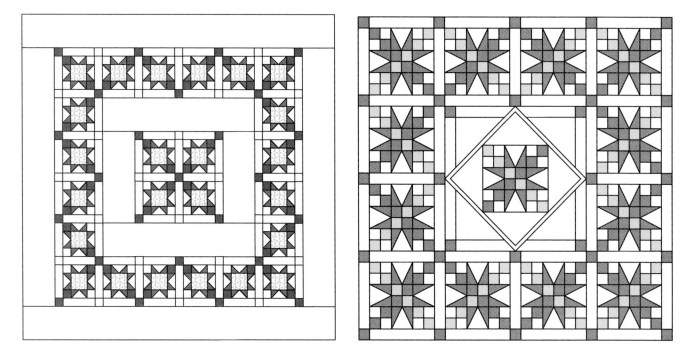

These settings include sashings and setting squares.

Design elements can be changed easily when working with graph and tracing paper. These two quilts start out with the same center design elements and show how the basic format can be changed from a square to a rectangle, with other elements changing as well.

These four Basket blocks, framed with sashing and setting squares, can stand on their own or form a center for a larger medallion setting by adding more borders.

This star setting could have four blocks in the center or one block set diagonally.

Designing Your Quilt

Equipment

As with any task, gathering your supplies and having a good work space with adequate lighting makes the job go more smoothly. Try to find a table or desk where you can leave your work in progress (also known as mess!) and come back to it whenever you have a few minutes or a new idea comes to mind. You will get a lot more done and use smaller bits of time if you don't have to get everything out each time you want to work and then put everything away when you are finished.

The following supplies are helpful when designing quilt settings.

Blocks

If you are starting with a stack of blocks, have them handy. You'll want to know how many you have, what their finished size is, and how true to size each block is. If your blocks vary in size more than ¼", you may want to design a setting where the blocks do not meet side by side.

Books, magazines, photos, quilt sketches

You'll find many examples of different setting possibilities on the pages of this book, but keep your eyes open for quilts that are set in ways that please you. Take your camera or a pad of paper to quilt shows and guild meetings to record settings that you like. When you are looking through quilt books or magazines that you own, tab pages that have appealing settings, using "sticky notes" or markers so you can find them easily.

Graph Paper

You'll find graph paper in notebook-sized tablets and in large single sheets (usually 17" x 22"). The smaller size is handy to carry with you for sketching, and the large sheets work well for planning large projects at home. The most common scale of graph paper is four squares to the inch, but it also comes five, six, and eight squares to the inch. These scales come in handy when you are working with blocks based on Ninepatch or twenty-five-patch grids and you want to draft blocks to scale. If you are working with blocks based on a Ninepatch, use graph paper with six squares to the inch so that the divisions in the block match up with the lines on the graph paper. When I'm working with a stack of blocks, I usually use a 1" or ½" square to represent the block and work out the size from there. Two sheets of graph paper (one for horizontal sets and one for diagonal sets) are included with this book for you to pull out and use.

Tracing Paper

Use this see-through paper over the top of graph paper for sketching quilt settings. This method not only saves graph paper but eliminates all the extra lines on the graph paper from interfering with the quilt design. It also makes it easier to include both horizontal and diagonal design elements in your sketch by changing the orientation of the graph paper under the tracing paper. This works especially well if you are planning a medallion-style setting, where the orientation of the blocks can change from horizontal to diagonal and back again.

See-Through Ruler

This 2" x 18" thin, clear acrylic ruler is useful for drafting designs and making templates. It is marked in inches with ⅛" divisions. These are not made to be used with a rotary cutter as they are too thin and the cutting blade will roll up on top of the ruler and ruin the edge. The 1" x 6" and 1" x 12" sizes are handy for sketching smaller shapes.

Lead Pencils

Mechanical pencils are preferable because they consistently give you a sharp, fine line, but any sharp pencils will work. Be sure to keep a good supply on hand.

Erasers

A big eraser is to sketching what the seam ripper is to sewing. Don't be without one!

Glue Stick

Anything sticky will do, but glue sticks are so easy to use.

Paper Scissors

Use these as you cut and paste designs together; don't use your good fabric scissors!

Colored Pencils or Markers

I use colored pencils to color in my design once it is sketched. I like a wide assortment of colors, either pencils or markers, but I find it easier to use pencils to get light and dark color variations.

Calculator

Since this process does involve some math, a calculator is helpful. Since a calculator gives you decimals and we're used to working in inches and fractions of inches in quiltmaking, you'll find a conversion chart on page 53.

Mirrors and Fresnell® Viewing Lenses

Two 12" square mirrors placed at right angles to each other can give you an idea of how your design will look repeated over and over again. Place the mirrors at the center of your design and see what happens. It's magic! Looking at a block through a Fresnell viewing lens repeats it over and over to give you a sense of its overall design.

Flannel Board

Placing your blocks on a flannel board or even a piece of batting tacked to the wall allows you to stand back and squint at your blocks and audition different arrangements, fabrics, borders, and sashing treatments. What looks wonderful on paper might not look so wonderful in real life, so this is a good way to test your ideas "in the flesh."

Designing on Paper

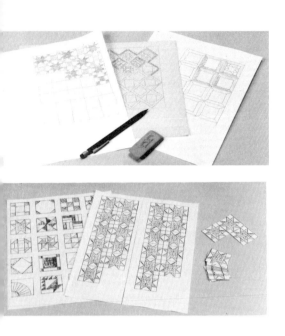

Step 1: By now, you have some idea of settings that you like. Your first sketches will probably be quite crude. Don't worry about using a ruler at this point. The main thing is to get your ideas down on paper—any kind of paper—before you forget them. I like starting out with the "paper-napkin approach," where you get the creativity flowing and focus on getting several possibilities down that you feel have some merit. Don't worry about being neat and tidy or coloring in your design. That can come later in the fine-tuning stage.

Step 2: Before going any further, you may want to sketch out your block design. If you are working with a pieced block, use graph paper in whichever scale matches your block. (See Graph Paper, page 44.) If you are making a large quilt with lots of repeating blocks, sketch your block so that 1½" is equal to one block. That way, graph paper that is divided into ⅛" squares will match up with a variety of blocks (including Ninepatch and sixteen-patch). If you are working with a complex block, a large block, or a block that doesn't repeat very much, use two or three inches to equal one block. This is really up to you and how big you want your working drawing to be; you will work out the scale later. Make enough copies of your block so that you can cut them out and arrange and rearrange them into various designs.

Step 3: Place a piece of tracing paper over your graph paper. Choose the horizontal or diagonal, depending on the orientation you are using. A few small pieces of tape will hold it in place. If you are planning a medallion-style setting where the orientation changes, start with the center orientation and retape your tracing paper onto the appropriate graph paper as you go along. Using your see-through ruler and a sharp lead pencil, sketch out your design, leaving blank spaces for your blocks so you can tape or glue copies of your block in place. This is the point where you can audition various options, such as different alternating blocks, framing ideas, or different sashing widths. If your quilt needs to be a predetermined size for a certain wall space or bed size, adjust the width of the sashings, frames, borders, or other components so your quilt will be the size required. For more information on bed sizes, see page 53. Use two mirrors or the Fresnell viewing lens (page 45) to see how your design will look repeated.

Step 4: When you are pleased with your design, tape or glue the copies of your block design into place. Make several copies of your finished design. Get out your colored pencils or markers and color in your design in various ways. Keep in mind that dark colors come forward while light colors tend to recede. If you want to use a strong color, try using it in smaller amounts so it won't overpower other parts of your design. This is your opportunity to try changing colors from the center to the edges of your design, or to try "floating" the blocks with sashing or alternating blocks. Don't forget that each set that you design has a number of color-choice possibilities. Finalize your setting design and color scheme.

Step 5: Using the size of your block as a guide, determine the size of the other parts of your setting. Make an inventory list of component parts that you will need to complete your top. Decide which fabrics will be used for each component of your design. Fill in the work sheet on page 51 with this information. This can be as detailed or as sketchy as you wish. By now, you will also have a good idea of the size of your quilt so you can determine how much fabric you will need for the binding and backing and what size batting you will need. Refer to the charts on pages 54–55 for help with the calculations.

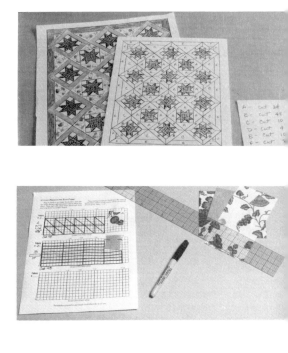

Step 6: The next step is to figure out how much of each fabric you need. Once you have decided which parts of your quilt will be cut from which fabric, use the fabric layout diagrams on page 52 and the chart on page 54 to calculate your fabric needs. You may duplicate the fabric layout diagrams to plan the yardage needed for each fabric. When I purchase fabric, I usually buy at least ½ yard extra to allow for mistakes and in case I change my color choices along the way. Planning a fabric layout for each of your main fabrics not only determines how much fabric you need but also the way to go about cutting it to best advantage. Begin by positioning the borders and long sashing strips along the lengthwise grain (which has less stretch) so you can avoid seaming strips together to get the correct length. Then fill in with smaller shapes. Check the chart on page 54 if you just have small shapes and no long strips. These diagrams are based on a fabric width of 40" of usable fabric after preshrinking, folded in half lengthwise. That means that each piece on your layout will yield two pieces when cut.

Step 7: You may want to make templates for any unusual shapes in your design. Cut them out of graph paper mounted on cardboard, X-ray film, or template plastic. Be sure to add a ¼"-wide seam allowance to each side. Most of the shapes you will be working with will be squares, rectangles, and triangles. To figure the cut size for squares and rectangles, add ½" to the length and width for seam allowances. There are two types of triangles and two ways of figuring out how to cut them.

Half-Square Triangles: These triangles are half of a square, with the short sides on the straight grain of fabric and the long side on the bias. To cut these triangles, cut a square and then cut it in half diagonally. *Cut the square ⅞" larger than the finished short side of the triangle to allow for seam allowances.* Each square makes two triangles.

Quarter-Square Triangles: Quarter-square triangles are usually used along the outside edges of blocks and quilts. Cut them from squares so their short sides are on the bias and the long side is on the straight of grain. This makes them easier to handle and keeps the outside edges of your quilt from stretching. *Cut the square 1¼" larger than the finished long side of the triangle to allow for seam allowances.* Each square makes four triangles.

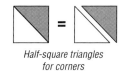

Half-square triangles for corners

Cut square 7/8" larger than finished size needed

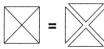

Quarter-square triangles for sides

Cut square 1 1/4" larger than finished size needed

Special Considerations

(or Situations You May Run Into That They Never Tell You About)

Let's take a look at several common problems you may run into when working with actual blocks, such as: setting blocks that aren't quite the same size, or setting unusual numbers of blocks together.

BLOCKS THAT AREN'T QUITE THE SAME SIZE

Often, no matter how hard you try, a set of blocks just doesn't end up all the same size. This often happens with sampler blocks or friendship blocks that are made by lots of different people. First, square up the blocks, using a 12" or 15" acrylic ruler and rotary cutter. Trim off the uneven parts along each side and try to end with all the blocks as close to the same size as possible.

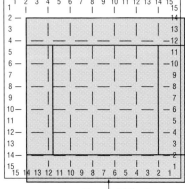

FUDGE TO FIT

If the difference in sizes ranges from no more than ⅛" to ¼", you will probably be able to join them, using the "Fudge to Fit" method.

1. If possible, arrange the blocks so that the smaller blocks are at the top of the quilt and the larger ones are at the bottom so less easing will be necessary.
2. As you piece the blocks together, place the smaller of the two blocks on top, right sides together. Pin the ends and any intersecting seams and points that need to match along the way. If things don't quite match up, you may need to decide which seams are going to show the most and match those and settle for "just close" on the others.
3. As you stitch the blocks together, keep the smaller one on top so that the feed dog on your sewing machine will pull more on the larger block and help to ease the small amount of excess into the seam. Hold onto each end of your blocks and pull gently to stretch them as they are stitched.

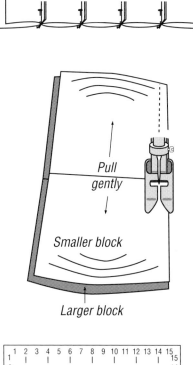

Pull gently

Smaller block

Larger block

FRAME TO FIT

Blocks that vary in size too much to be fudged together can be standardized in size by adding a frame around them. Decide on the approximate width of the frame, adding ½" for seam allowances, plus another ½"–1" (for trimming), depending on the difference in size between the smallest and largest blocks. The wider the frame, the less the difference in size will show. Some frames that work well for squaring up blocks are noted in the framed block section on page 33. After stitching the frames onto the blocks, use a 12" or 15" acrylic square to trim them all down to a uniform size. Center the block in the frame and trim away an equal amount from each side of the frames.

Framed block

Another option is to add oversized triangles around your blocks. Then trim the resulting blocks to a standard size. If the fabric you use is the same as the background fabric in the blocks, the blocks will appear to float. The framed blocks can be set horizontally or diagonally.

Adding oversized triangles that are the same fabric as the block background makes the design appear to float.

THE MEDALLION CONNECTION

If most of your blocks are the same size with only a few oddballs to worry about, consider a medallion setting.

1. Stitch together either the four largest or four smallest blocks for the center medallion. Hopefully, the remaining blocks will be fairly close in size.
2. Frame the medallion with borders or corner triangles, or both.
3. Add the remaining blocks around the edges. Look through the Medallion section on pages 41–43 for additional ideas.

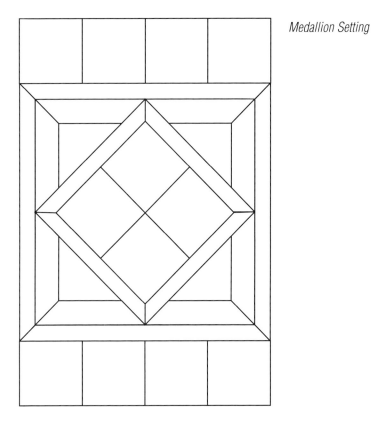

Medallion Setting

HOW TO SET AN UNUSUAL NUMBER OF BLOCKS

It's easy to figure how to set thirty blocks together. You can easily set them in six rows with five blocks in each row, but what do you do with twenty-six blocks? Thirteen rows of two blocks in each row isn't too practical. An odd number of blocks, such as seven or seventeen, also presents a challenge. There are several solutions to consider.

Alternating Plain or Design Blocks

When a main block alternates with another block, they are usually set with an odd number of blocks and an odd number of rows so that the same block will end up in each corner.

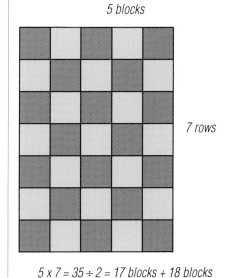

5 blocks

7 rows

5 x 7 = 35 ÷ 2 = 17 blocks + 18 blocks

If you multiply the odd number of blocks in a row by the odd number of rows, you will end up with an odd number of total blocks needed. Now divide the total number of blocks needed in two equal groups and you will have one group with one more block than the other. Perhaps the number of blocks you have will work into one of the following arrangements:

Blocks Across	Rows Down	No. of A Blocks	No. of B Blocks	Total No. of Blocks
3	5	7	8	15
5	7	17	18	35
7	9	31	32	63
9	11	49	50	99

Diagonal Settings

Diagonal settings, with blocks set side by side or with alternating blocks, can also accommodate an unusual number of blocks. If your blocks are oriented horizontally, add corner-triangle framing around them to change them to a diagonal orientation. A good example of this is "Class Heroes" (page 28) where twenty-six students made blocks to be set together. Here are some other possibilities:

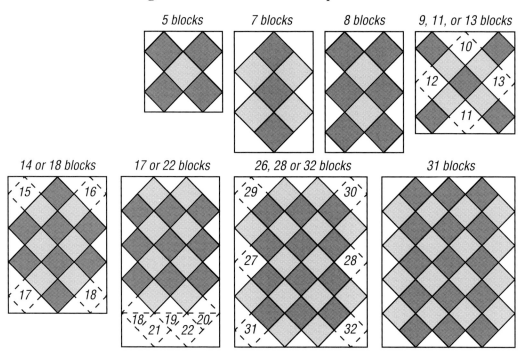

Medallions

A medallion setting might be the answer for setting an unusual number of blocks. Take another look at some of the medallion settings on pages 41–43 and the number of blocks in each.

Don't Forget the Border

If you have four blocks too many, plan a border the same width as your blocks and put one in each corner. If you still have one left over, incorporate it into your label on the back of the quilt.

Set Design Work Sheet and Inventory

Fill out this work sheet in as much detail as you wish. Use the completed work sheet, along with the fabric layout diagrams, to determine how much of each fabric you will need to complete your quilt, including the binding, batting, and backing. Not all categories will apply to each quilt, but you can organize each component of your quilt and record which fabric you plan to use for each. Use the reference charts, beginning on page 53, to determine your fabric requirements. The goal is to complete the section below so you can go fabric shopping!

Type of Setting _____

Finished Size of Quilt _____

Block Design _____

Size of Block _____

Additional notes:

Fabric #

Number of Main Blocks _____ _____

Number of Alternating Blocks _____ _____

Number of Sashing Strips (Short) _____ _____

Number of Sashing Strips (Long) _____ _____

Number of Setting Squares _____ _____

Number of Side Triangles _____ _____

Corner Triangles _____ _____

First Border _____ _____

Second Border _____ _____

Third Border _____ _____

Binding _____ _____

Backing _____ _____

Yardage Needed for Each Fabric: (Use the fabric cutting layout diagrams on page 52 to help you estimate your yardage requirements.)

Fabric #1: | Swatch | Yardage ____

Fabric #2: | Swatch | Yardage ____

Fabric #3: | Swatch | Yardage ____

Fabric #4: | Swatch | Yardage ____

Fabric #5: | Swatch | Yardage ____

Fabric #6: | Swatch | Yardage ____

CUTTING DIAGRAM FOR EACH FABRIC

Plug in borders and large blocks first. (Run border strips along lengthwise grain of fabric when possible.) Then start with other large pieces and work your way down to smaller shapes.

These cutting layouts are based on a 40" width of usable fabric, folded in half, so you will be cutting two of each piece. Each ☐ = 2".

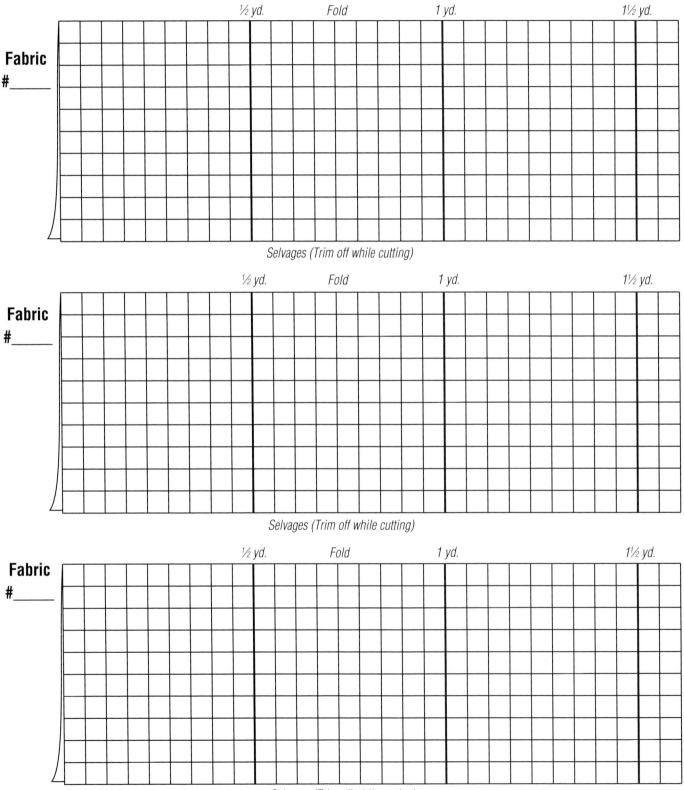

Fabric #_____

½ yd.   Fold   1 yd.   1½ yd.

Selvages (Trim off while cutting)

Fabric #_____

½ yd.   Fold   1 yd.   1½ yd.

Selvages (Trim off while cutting)

Fabric #_____

½ yd.   Fold   1 yd.   1½ yd.

Selvages (Trim off while cutting)

52   Permission granted to photocopy work sheet for your use.

Quick Reference Charts

This section contains charts and other references to help simplify many of the common calculations you will need when designing quilts.

COMMON BED SIZES

If you are designing a quilt for a specific bed, it is best to measure the actual bed, but if this isn't possible, use the chart below.

Bed	Mattress Size
Crib	23" x 46"
Youth	32" x 66"
Twin	39" x 75"
Double	54" x 75"
Queen	60" x 80"
King	78" x 80"
Calif. King	72" x 84"

DECIMAL TO INCH CONVERSIONS

When you are using a calculator, you will run into fractions given as decimals. Use this chart to convert them to fractions or to round them off to the nearest ⅛".

.125	=	⅛"
.25	=	¼"
.375	=	⅜"
.50	=	½"
.625	=	⅝"
.75	=	¾"
.875	=	⅞"
1.0	=	1"

DIAGONAL MEASUREMENTS OF STANDARD-SIZE BLOCKS

When you set blocks diagonally, it is helpful to know the diagonal measurement of the block so that you can figure the quilt size. To figure this yourself, multiply the length of one side of the block by 1.414, or use the chart below.

2" block	=	2⅞"
3" block	=	4¼"
4" block	=	5⅝"
5" block	=	7⅛"
6" block	=	8½"
7" block	=	9⅞"
8" block	=	11¼"
9" block	=	12¾"
10" block	=	14⅛"
12" block	=	17"
14" block	=	19⅞"
16" block	=	22⅝"
18" block	=	25½"
20" block	=	28¼"
24" block	=	34"

Diagonal Measurment

CALCULATING CORNER AND SIDE TRIANGLES

It is important to cut corner and side triangles so that the grain lines run vertically and horizontally. This stabilizes the quilt, prevents sagging, and makes the borders go on more smoothly.

Corner Triangles

Corner triangles are made from a square cut diagonally in one direction so that one square yields two corner triangles. To calculate the size of square needed, divide the finished block size by 1.414 and add .875" (⅞") for seam allowances. Round this up to the nearest ⅛".

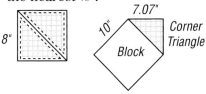

10" ÷ 1.414 = 7.07 + .875 = 7.95" or 8"

Side Triangles

Side triangles are made from a square cut diagonally in two directions so that one square yields four side triangles. To calculate the size of square needed, multiply the finished block size by 1.414 and add 1.25" (1¼") for seam allowances. Round this up to the nearest ⅛".

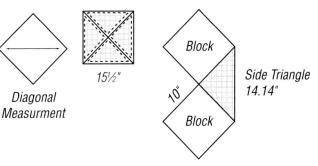

10" x 1.414 = 14.14" + 1.25 = 15.39" or 15½"

The following chart gives you the measurements for side and corner triangles for the most common quilt-block sizes. However, you may overcut your squares by ½"–1" and trim them down once your top is pieced together.

Finished Block Size	Cut Square Size for Corner Triangle	Cut Square Size for Side Triangle
2" Block	2⅜"	4⅛"
3" Block	3"	5½"
4" Block	3¾"	7"
5" Block	4½"	8⅜"
6" Block	5⅛"	9¾"
7" Block	5⅞"	11¼"
8" Block	6⅝"	12⅝"
9" Block	7¼"	14"
10" Block	8"	15½"
12" Block	9⅜"	18¼"
14" Block	10⅞"	21⅛"
16" Block	12¼"	23⅞"
18" Block	13⅝"	26¾"
20" Block	15⅛"	29⅝"
24" Block	17⅞"	35¼"

ESTIMATING YARDAGE REQUIREMENTS

The following chart is based on a 40" width of fabric. Most 100% cotton fabrics used for quiltmaking are between 42"–44" wide, but after preshrinking and trimming off the selvages, I consider anything over 40" a bonus. So, you might get a few more pieces than I have estimated, but you won't come up short.

Even though this chart only gives yardage requirements for squares, it can easily be used for other shapes. For half-square triangles, multiply the number of squares by two. For quarter-square triangles, multiply the number of squares by four.

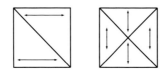

Arrows indicate straight of grain

For rectangles, figure how many will fit into a square and calculate from there.

Two rectangles　　　*Three rectangles*

For irregular shapes, figure how many will fit into a certain size square and go from there.

YARDAGE CHART FOR SQUARES

Size of Square		Yardage Needed (40" of usable fabric)							
cut	finished	¼ yd.	½ yd.	¾ yd.	1 yd.	1¼ yds.	1½ yds.	1¾ yds.	2 yds.
1½"	1"	130	286	416	572	702	858	1066	1144
2"	1½"	80	160	240	320	400	480	620	640
2½"	2"	48	96	160	224	272	320	400	448
3"	2½"	26	65	104	143	195	221	260	286
3½"	3"	22	55	77	110	132	165	187	220
4"	3½"	20	40	60	80	110	130	150	170
4½"	4"	8	27	40	56	72	88	104	112
5"	4½"	8	24	40	56	64	80	96	112
5½"	5"	7	21	28	42	56	63	77	84
6"	5½"	6	12	24	30	42	48	60	66
6½"	6"	6	12	24	30	36	48	54	66
7½"	7"	5	10	15	20	25	35	40	45
8½"	8"	4	8	12	16	20	24	28	32
9½"	9"		4	8	12	16	20	24	28
10½"	10"		3	6	9	12	15	15	18
11½"	11"		3	6	9	9	12	15	18
12½"	12"		3	6	6	9	12	15	15
13½"	13"		2	4	4	6	8	8	10
14½"	14"		2	2	4	6	6	8	8
15½"	15"		2	2	4	4	6	8	8
16½"	16"		2	2	4	4	6	6	8
17½"	17"		2	2	4	4	6	6	8
18½"	18"			2	2	4	4	6	6
19½"	19"			2	2	4	4	6	6

YARDAGE REQUIREMENTS FOR BINDING

The yardage requirements given here are based on a binding that is made from a 2"-wide strip of fabric. Decide if you want to cut your strips on the straight of grain or on the bias. Bias strips take slightly more fabric; however, the yardage given is ample for either one. Binding strips cut 2" wide can be used for a traditional single-layer binding with a finished width of ½".

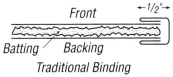

Front ←1/2"→

Batting   Backing
Traditional Binding

For a double-layer French binding, fold 2¼"-wide strips in half lengthwise, wrong sides together. Then stitch the raw edges to the quilt and the remaining folded edge to the back of the quilt. The finished width will be ⅜".

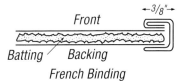

Front ←3/8"→

Batting   Backing
French Binding

Determine the distance around your quilt and add about 20" for turning the corners and for seaming the binding strips together into one continuous piece. Round this number up to the nearest yard to determine the length of the binding strip.

Length of Binding	Fabric Needed
4 yds.	¼ yd. *
6 yds.	⅓ yd.
8 yds.	½ yd.
10 yds.	⅔ yd.
12 yds.	¾ yd.
16 yds.	1 yd.

It is a good idea to purchase ½ yard of fabric instead of ¼ yard so the binding pieces will be longer and won't require as many joining seams to make the continuous strip.

YARDAGE REQUIREMENTS FOR BACKING

The backing for most quilts larger than crib size will need to be pieced together from two or more strips of fabric if 42"-wide fabric is used. The piecing seams can run horizontally or vertically in the backing, as long as the fabric isn't a directional print. Look for 90"-wide 100% cotton in solid colors to back large quilts without the necessity of piecing seams. Avoid the temptation to use a bed sheet for a backing as it is difficult to quilt through.

If you are planning to put a sleeve or rod pocket on the back of your quilt so you can hang it, purchase a little extra backing fabric so that the sleeve and the backing match. Once you know the finished size of your quilt, refer to the following diagrams to plan how to lay out the backing and determine how much fabric is required. Be sure to trim off the selvages on the seams.

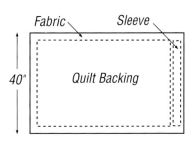

Fabric   Sleeve

Quilt Backing

40"

Up to 40" width or length
Example: 60" (length or width) + 18" (½ yd. for trimming and sleeve) = 78" (2⅛ yds.)

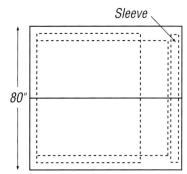

Sleeve

80"

Up to 80" width or length
Example: 2 x 100" (length or width) = 200" + 27" (¾ yd. for trimming and sleeve) = 227" (6⅓ yds.)

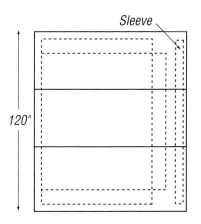

Sleeve

120"

Up to 120" width or length
Example: 3 x 100" = 300" + 36" (1 yd. for trimming and sleeve) = 336" (9⅓ yds.)

That Patchwork Place Publications and Products

BOOKS

All the Blocks Are Geese by Mary Sue Suit
Angle Antics by Mary Hickey
Animas Quilts by Jackie Robinson
Appliqué Borders: An Added Grace by Jeana Kimball
Baltimore Bouquets by Mimi Dietrich
Basket Garden by Mary Hickey
Biblical Blocks by Rosemary Makhan
Blockbuster Quilts by Margaret J. Miller
Calendar Quilts by Joan Hanson
Cathedral Window: A Fresh Look by Nancy J. Martin
Corners in the Cabin by Paulette Peters
Country Medallion Sampler by Carol Doak
Country Threads by Connie Tesene and Mary Tendall
Easy Machine Paper Piecing by Carol Doak
Even More by Trudie Hughes
Fantasy Flowers: Pieced Flowers for Quilters
    by Doreen Cronkite Burbank
Feathered Star Sampler by Marsha McCloskey
Fit To Be Tied by Judy Hopkins
Five- and Seven-Patch Blocks & Quilts for the ScrapSaver™
    by Judy Hopkins
Four-Patch Blocks & Quilts for the ScrapSaver™
    by Judy Hopkins
Fun with Fat Quarters by Nancy J. Martin
Go Wild with Quilts: 14 North American Birds and Animals
    by Margaret Rolfe
Handmade Quilts by Mimi Dietrich
Happy Endings—Finishing the Edges of Your Quilt
    by Mimi Dietrich
Holiday Happenings by Christal Carter
Home for Christmas by Nancy J. Martin and Sharon Stanley
In The Beginning by Sharon Evans Yenter
Jacket Jazz by Judy Murrah
Lessons in Machine Piecing by Marsha McCloskey
Little By Little: Quilts in Miniature by Mary Hickey
Little Quilts by Alice Berg, Sylvia Johnson, and
    Mary Ellen Von Holt
Lively Little Logs by Donna McConnell
Loving Stitches: A Guide to Fine Hand Quilting
    by Jeana Kimball
More Template-Free™ *Quiltmaking* by Trudie Hughes
Nifty Ninepatches by Carolann M. Palmer
Nine-Patch Blocks & Quilts for the ScrapSaver™
    by Judy Hopkins
Not Just Quilts by Jo Parrott
On to Square Two by Marsha McCloskey
Osage County Quilt Factory by Virginia Robertson
Painless Borders by Sally Schneider
A Perfect Match: A Guide to Precise Machine Piecing
    by Donna Lynn Thomas

Picture Perfect Patchwork by Naomi Norman
Piecemakers® *Country Store* by the Piecemakers
Pineapple Passion by Nancy Smith and Lynda Milligan
A Pioneer Doll and Her Quilts by Mary Hickey
Pioneer Storybook Quilts by Mary Hickey
Quick & Easy Quiltmaking: 26 Projects Featuring Speedy
    Cutting and Piecing Methods by Mary Hickey,
    Nancy J. Martin, Marsha McCloskey & Sara Nephew
Quilts for All Seasons: Year-Round Log Cabin Designs
    by Christal Carter
Quilts for Baby: Easy as A, B, C by Ursula Reikes
Quilts for Kids by Carolann M. Palmer
Quilts from Nature by Joan Colvin
Quilts to Share by Janet Kime
Red and Green: An Appliqué Tradition by Jeana Kimball
Red Wagon Originals by Gerry Kimmel and Linda Brannock
Rotary Riot: 40 Fast & Fabulous Quilts by Judy Hopkins
    and Nancy J. Martin
Rotary Roundup: 40 More Fast & Fabulous Quilts by Judy
    Hopkins and Nancy J. Martin
Round About Quilts by J. Michelle Watts
Samplings from the Sea by Rosemary Makhan
Scrap Happy by Sally Schneider
Sensational Settings: Over 80 Ways to Arrange Your Quilt
    Blocks by Joan Hanson
Sewing on the Line: Fast and Easy Foundation Piecing
    by Lesly-Claire Greenberg
Shortcuts: A Concise Guide to Rotary Cutting
    by Donna Lynn Thomas (metric version available)
Small Talk by Donna Lynn Thomas
Smoothstitch™ *Quilts: Easy Machine Appliqué*
    by Roxi Eppler
The Stitchin' Post by Jean Wells and Lawry Thorn
Strips That Sizzle by Margaret J. Miller
Tea Party Time: Romantic Quilts and Tasty Tidbits
    by Nancy J. Martin
Template-Free™ *Quiltmaking* by Trudie Hughes
Template-Free™ *Quilts and Borders* by Trudie Hughes
Template-Free® *Stars* by Jo Parrott
Watercolor Quilts by Pat Maixner Magaret and
    Donna Ingram Slusser
Women and Their Quilts by Nancyann Johanson Twelker

TOOLS

6" Bias Square®	Rotary Mate™
8" Bias Square®	Rotary Rule™
Metric Bias Square®	Ruby Beholder™
BiRangle™	ScrapSaver™
Pineapple Rule	

VIDEO

Shortcuts to America's Best-Loved Quilts

Many titles are available at your local quilt shop. For more information, send $2 for a color catalog to That Patchwork Place, Inc., PO Box 118, Bothell WA 98041-0118 USA.

☎ Call 1-800-426-3126 for the name and location of the quilt shop nearest you.